PIANO

Adventures® *by Nancy and Randall Faber*

THE BASIC PIANO METHOD

_____ is sightreading this book!

(your name)

Production Coordinator: Jon Ophoff
Cover: Terpstra Design, San Francisco
Illustrations: Erika LeBarre

ISBN 978-1-61677-630-5
Copyright © 2011 Dovetree Productions, Inc.
c/o FABER PIANO ADVENTURES, 3042 Creek Dr., Ann Arbor, MI 48108.
International Copyright Secured. All Rights Reserved. Printed in U.S.A.

CHART YOUR PROGRESS

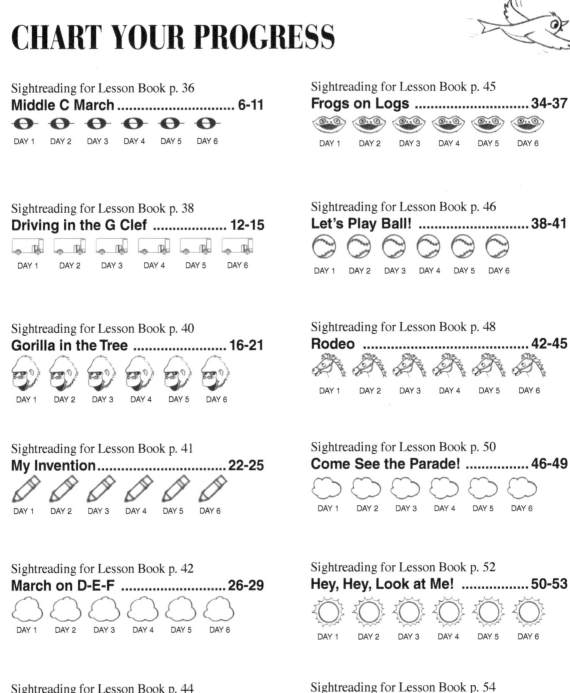

Sightreading for Lesson Book p. 36
Middle C March 6-11

DAY 1   DAY 2   DAY 3   DAY 4   DAY 5   DAY 6

Sightreading for Lesson Book p. 38
Driving in the G Clef 12-15

DAY 1   DAY 2   DAY 3   DAY 4   DAY 5   DAY 6

Sightreading for Lesson Book p. 40
Gorilla in the Tree 16-21

DAY 1   DAY 2   DAY 3   DAY 4   DAY 5   DAY 6

Sightreading for Lesson Book p. 41
My Invention 22-25

DAY 1   DAY 2   DAY 3   DAY 4   DAY 5   DAY 6

Sightreading for Lesson Book p. 42
March on D-E-F 26-29

DAY 1   DAY 2   DAY 3   DAY 4   DAY 5   DAY 6

Sightreading for Lesson Book p. 44
The Dance Band 30-33

DAY 1   DAY 2   DAY 3   DAY 4   DAY 5   DAY 6

Sightreading for Lesson Book p. 45
Frogs on Logs 34-37

DAY 1   DAY 2   DAY 3   DAY 4   DAY 5   DAY 6

Sightreading for Lesson Book p. 46
Let's Play Ball! 38-41

DAY 1   DAY 2   DAY 3   DAY 4   DAY 5   DAY 6

Sightreading for Lesson Book p. 48
Rodeo 42-45

DAY 1   DAY 2   DAY 3   DAY 4   DAY 5   DAY 6

Sightreading for Lesson Book p. 50
Come See the Parade! 46-49

DAY 1   DAY 2   DAY 3   DAY 4   DAY 5   DAY 6

Sightreading for Lesson Book p. 52
Hey, Hey, Look at Me! 50-53

DAY 1   DAY 2   DAY 3   DAY 4   DAY 5   DAY 6

Sightreading for Lesson Book p. 54
Elephant Ride 54-57

DAY 1   DAY 2   DAY 3   DAY 4   DAY 5   DAY 6

Sightreading for Lesson Book p. 55
Yankee Doodle **58-61**

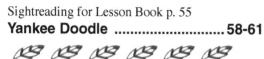

DAY 1   DAY 2   DAY 3   DAY 4   DAY 5   DAY 6

Sightreading for Lesson Book p. 57
A Joke for You **62-65**

DAY 1   DAY 2   DAY 3   DAY 4   DAY 5   DAY 6

Sightreading for Lesson Book p. 58
Football Game **66-69**

DAY 1   DAY 2   DAY 3   DAY 4   DAY 5   DAY 6

Sightreading for Lesson Book p. 60
Copy Cat **70-73**

DAY 1   DAY 2   DAY 3   DAY 4   DAY 5   DAY 6

Sightreading for Lesson Book p. 62
Grandmother **74-77**

DAY 1   DAY 2   DAY 3   DAY 4   DAY 5   DAY 6

Sightreading for Lesson Book p. 64
Lemonade Stand **78-81**

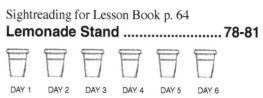

DAY 1   DAY 2   DAY 3   DAY 4   DAY 5   DAY 6

Sightreading for Lesson Book p. 66
All My Friends **82-85**

DAY 1   DAY 2   DAY 3   DAY 4   DAY 5   DAY 6

Sightreading for Lesson Book p. 69
Princess or Monster? **86-89**

DAY 1   DAY 2   DAY 3   DAY 4   DAY 5   DAY 6

Sightreading for Lesson Book p. 70
The Bugle Boys **90-95**

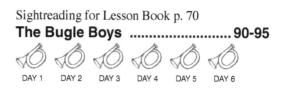

DAY 1   DAY 2   DAY 3   DAY 4   DAY 5   DAY 6

Certificate of Completion **96**

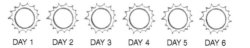

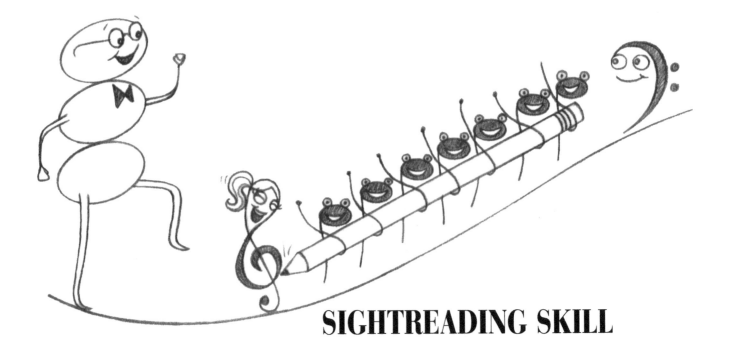

SIGHTREADING SKILL

Good sightreading skill is a powerful asset for the developing musician. It makes every step of music-making easier. With the right tools and a little work, sightreading skill can be developed to great benefit.

This book builds confident readers in two ways: 1) recognition of individual notes, and 2) perception of note patterns, both rhythmic and melodic.

In language literacy, the reader must not only identify single words, but also group words together for understanding. Similarly, music reading involves more than note naming. The sightreader tracks horizontally and vertically, observing intervals and contour while gleaning familiar patterns that make up the musical context.

This decoding skill requires repetition within familiar musical contexts. In other words, pattern recognition develops by seeing a lot of the same patterns. Accordingly, this book presents musical variations to sharpen  perception of the new against a backdrop of the familiar. To use the literacy analogy, the musician must not only identify single notes, but also group notes into musical patterns for understanding.

SIGHTREADING

How to Use

This book is organized into sets of 6 exercises, for 6 days of practice. Each set provides variations on a piece from the **Piano Adventures® Primer Level Lesson Book.** Play one exercise a day, completing one set per week.

Though the student is not required to repeatedly "practice" the sightreading exercise, each should be repeated once or twice as indicated by the repeat sign. For an extra workout, play each of the previous exercises in the set before playing the new exercise of the day.

Curiosity and Fun

The "Don't Practice This!" motto is a bold statement which has an obvious psychological impact. It reminds us that sightreading is indeed "the first time through" and it reminds us to keep the activity fun.

The comic-style illustrations ("educational art") draw students through consecutive pages by stimulating curiosity. Little Treble, Little Bass, Penny Piano, Freddie Forte, Buddy Barline and other characters captivate the beginning reader with musical questions, antics and requests. Each page presents a new "learning vignette" in a spirit of fun.

⌐DON'T
PRACTICE
THIS!⌐

Level of Difficulty

It is most beneficial to sightread at the appropriate level of difficulty. Some experts say that a child should not stumble on more than three or four words per page when learning to read. Similarly, a sightreader should not stumble on more than three or four notes per page. This Piano Adventures® Sightreading Book is carefully written to match the Primer level of difficulty and to provide appropriate challenge.

Marking Progress

Students are encouraged to draw a large **X** over each completed exercise. This instruction is so out of the ordinary that students find it immensely satisfying to mark their progress in this way.

Additionally, students wishing to celebrate the completion of a set may color the illustration of Day 6.

Some students may exclaim about the thickness of the book! They soon are rewarded to find how fast they can move through it. Indeed, with confidence increasing, the student can take pride in moving to completion of this very large book…and do so with a crescendo of achievement.

Instructions to Student

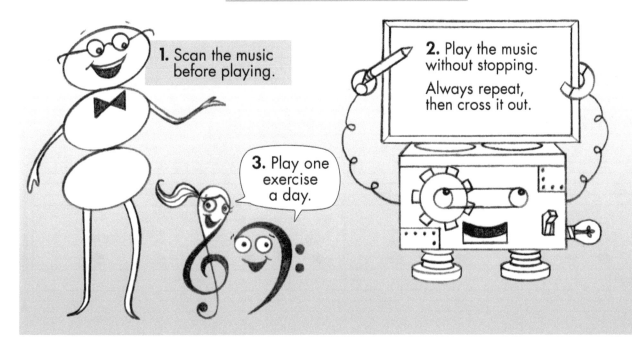

1. Scan the music before playing.

2. Play the music without stopping.

Always repeat, then cross it out.

3. Play one exercise a day.

DAY 1: Middle C March

DON'T PRACTICE THIS!

Notice the finger change at the end of each line.

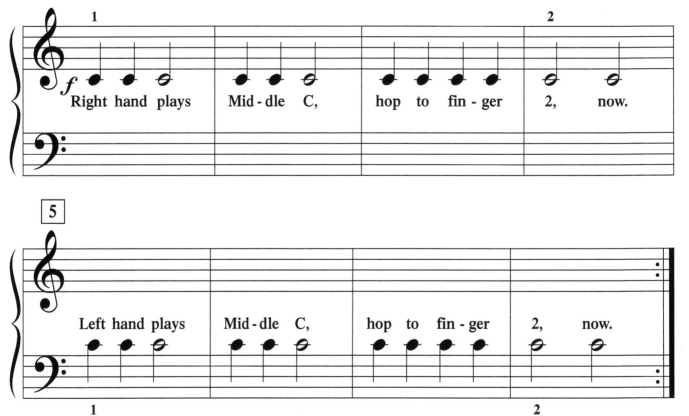

DAY 2: Middle C March

Which finger begins? Where does it change?

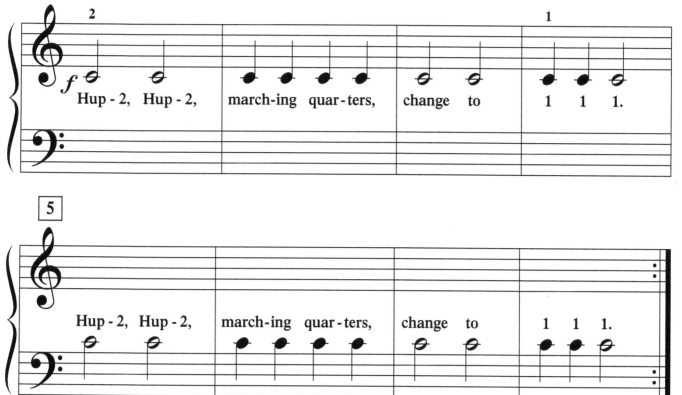

DAY 3: Middle C March

DON'T PRACTICE THIS!

Notice the finger change at the end of each line.

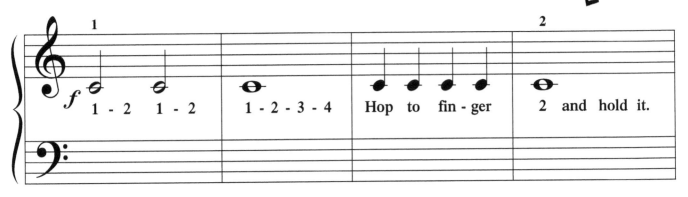

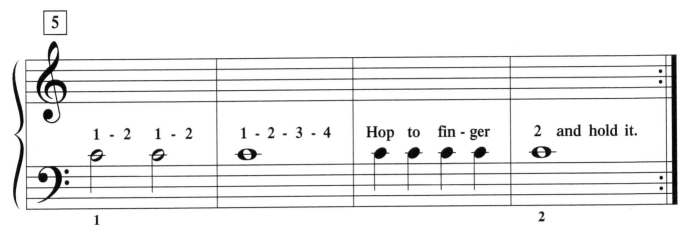

Hey, piano friend! I'm marching to your beat. Don't forget to count **1-2-3-4** for the whole notes. Way to go!

Remember, after you sightread, put a **BIG X** across the music.

DAY 4: Middle C March

DON'T PRACTICE THIS!

Which finger begins? Where does it change?

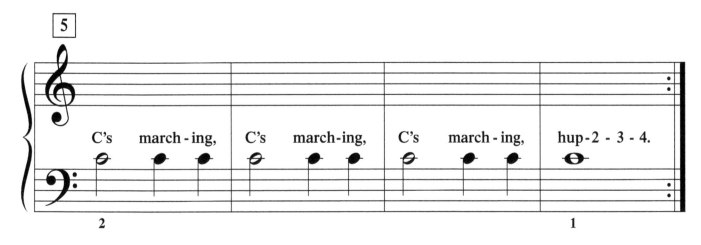

WHO IS RIGHT?

DAY 5: Middle C March

DON'T PRACTICE THIS!

Notice the finger changes.

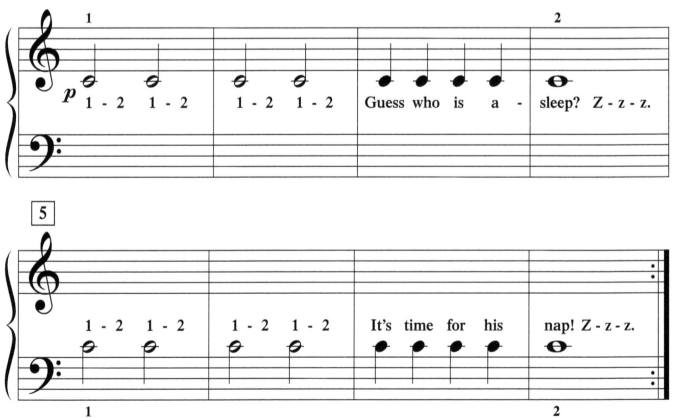

DAY 6: Middle C March

DON'T PRACTICE THIS!

Notice the quick change from *f* to *p*.

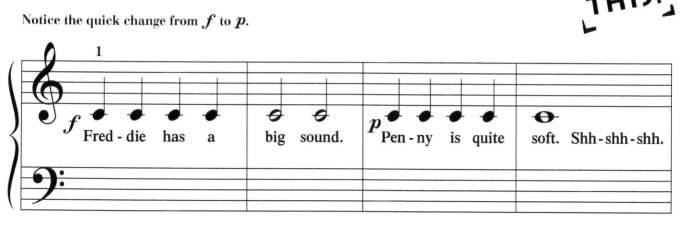

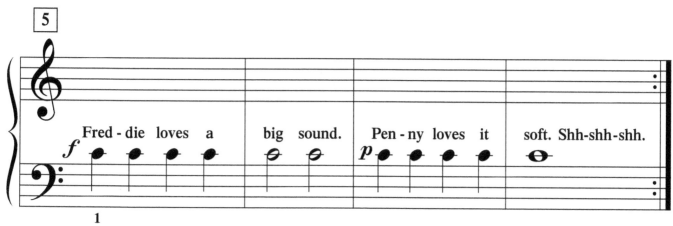

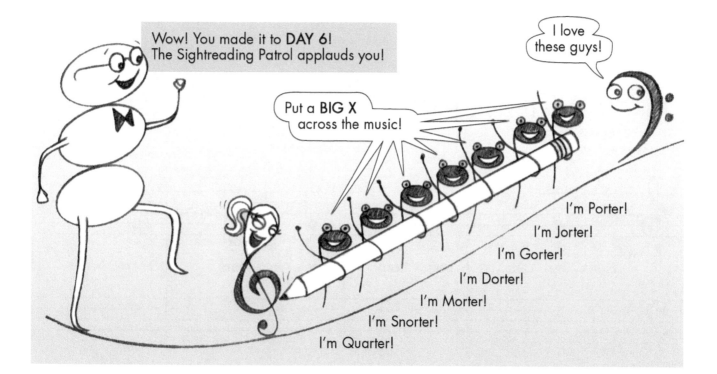

Which Chord Guy looks like the first measure of **DAY 1**?

or   or

DAY 1: Driving in the G Clef

DON'T PRACTICE THIS!

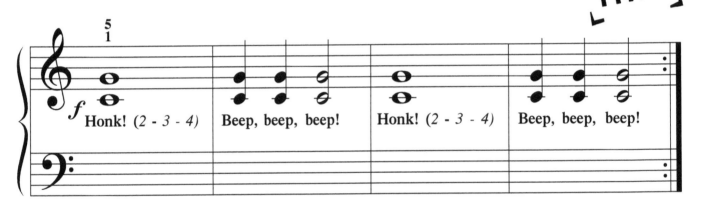

f Honk! (2 - 3 - 4) | Beep, beep, beep! | Honk! (2 - 3 - 4) | Beep, beep, beep!

DAY 2: Driving in the G Clef

What does *mf* mean? _____

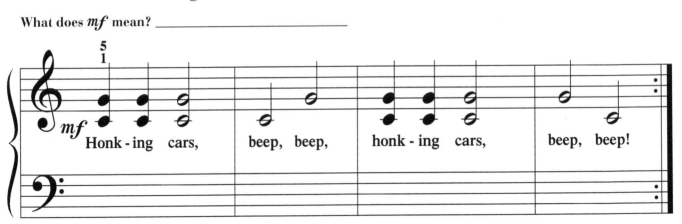

mf Honk - ing cars, | beep, beep, | honk - ing cars, | beep, beep!

DAY 3: Driving in the G Clef

DON'T PRACTICE THIS!

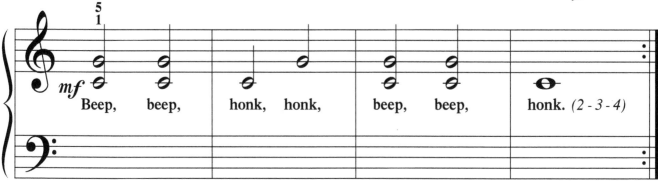

Beep, beep,   honk, honk,   beep, beep,   honk. *(2 - 3 - 4)*

DAY 4: Driving in the G Clef

Notice the quick change from *f* to *p*.

Honk, honk!   Beep, beep!   Horns are soft - er   now. *(2 - 3 - 4)*

I think I just saw Little Treble and Little Bass speed by in a honking car. Did you see them?

How well can you spot half notes? On this page, put a ✓ above 5 measures with **only** half notes.

13

DAY 5: Driving in the G Clef

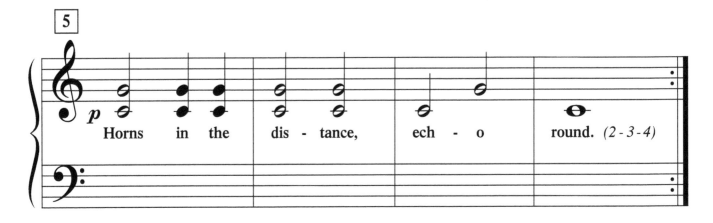

DAY 6: Driving in the G Clef

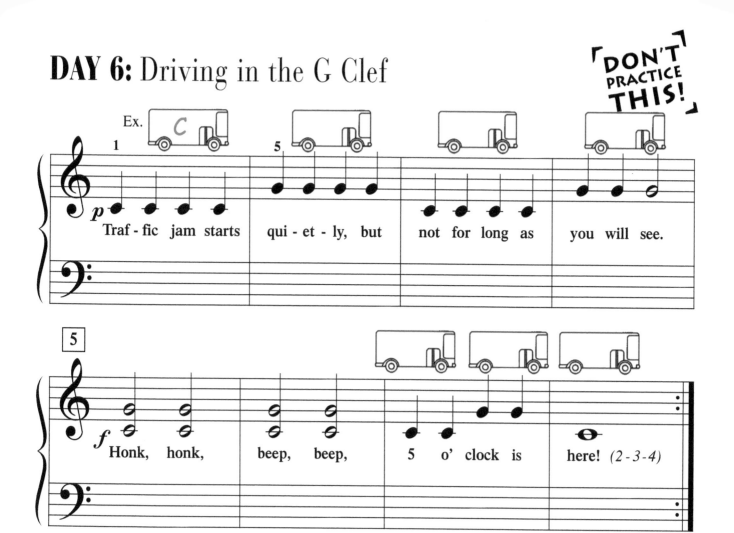

DAY 1: Gorilla in the Tree

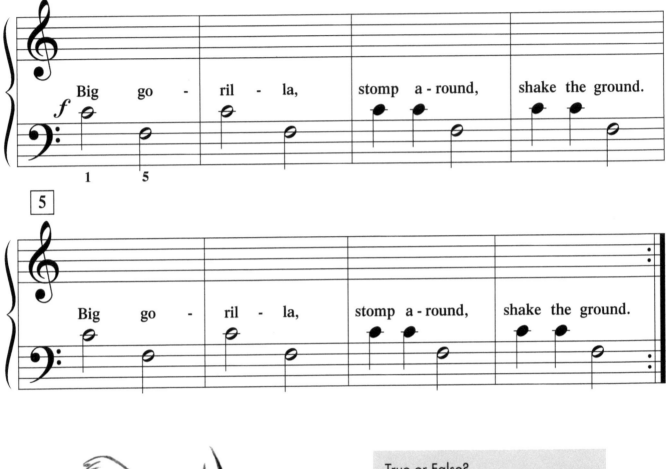

DAY 2: Gorilla in the Tree

17

DAY 3: Gorilla in the Tree

DAY 4: Gorilla in the Tree

DAY 5: Gorilla in the Tree

DON'T PRACTICE THIS!

DAY 6: Middle C March

DON'T PRACTICE THIS!

Notice the quick change from *f* to *p*.

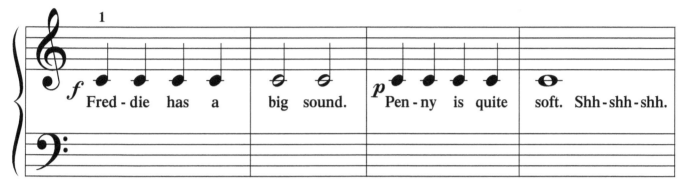

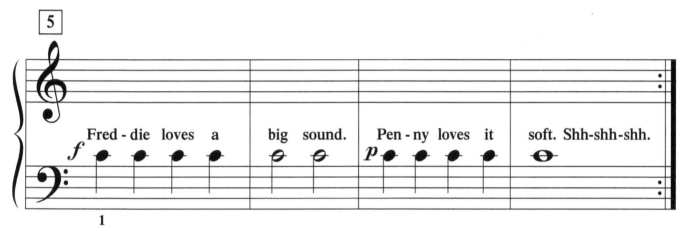

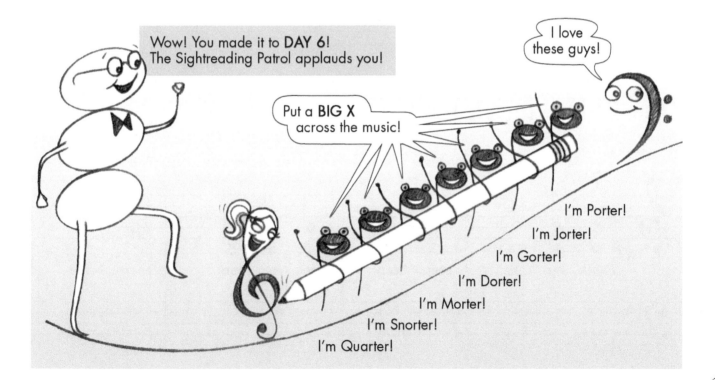

Which Chord Guy looks like the first measure of **DAY 1**?

DAY 1: Driving in the G Clef

DON'T PRACTICE **THIS!**

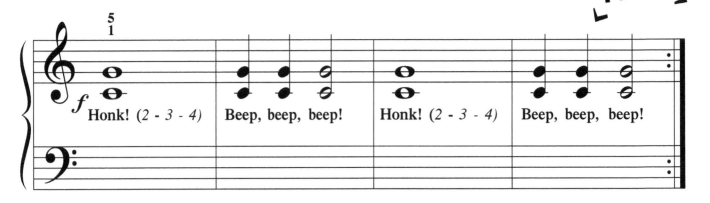

DAY 2: Driving in the G Clef

What does *mf* mean? _____

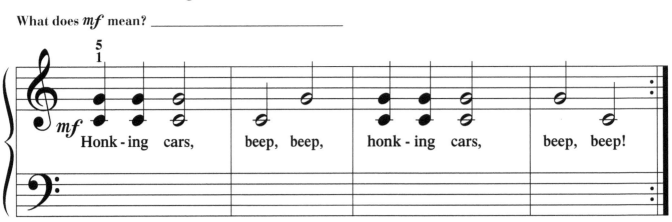

DAY 6: Gorilla in the Tree

DON'T PRACTICE THIS!

21

DAY 1: My Invention

Notice the starting L.H. finger.

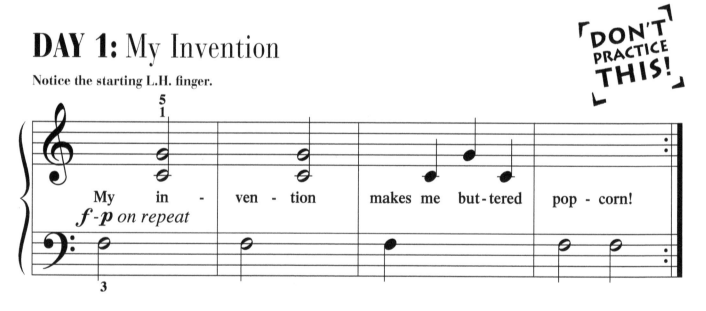

My in - ven - tion makes me but-tered pop-corn!

f-p on repeat

DAY 2: My Invention

It can talk, it can walk, my in-ven-tion's great!

mf

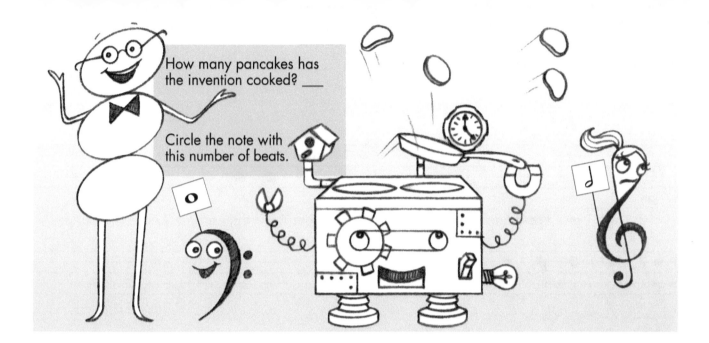

DAY 3: My Invention

Notice the starting L.H. finger.

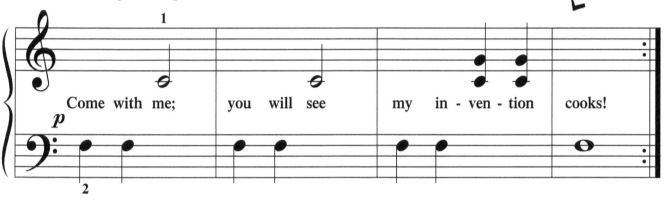

DAY 4: My Invention

Notice the quick change from *f* to *p*.

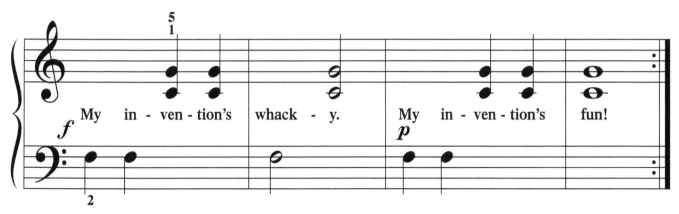

DAY 5: My Invention

DAY 6: My Invention

DAY 1: March on D-E-F

Can you sing as you play?

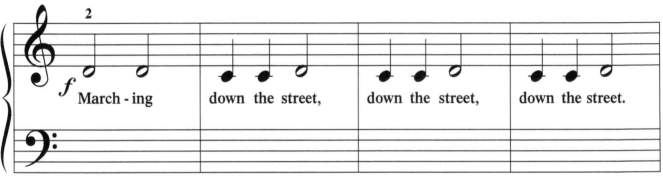

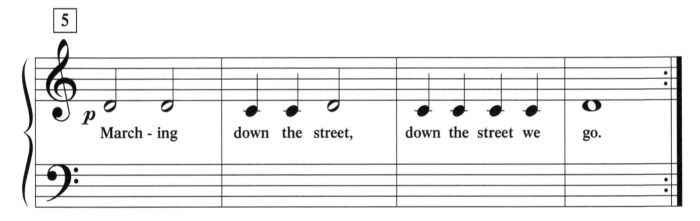

DAY 2: March on D-E-F

Can you sing the note names as you play?

DAY 3: March on D-E-F

Notice the starting finger.

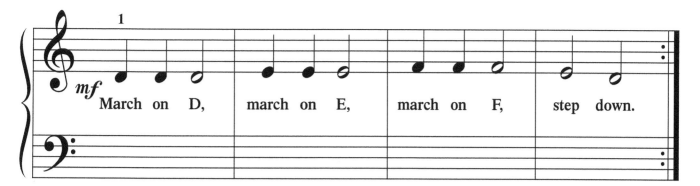

WHO IS CORRECT? (circle one)

DAY 4: March on D-E-F

Notice the starting finger.

DON'T PRACTICE THIS!

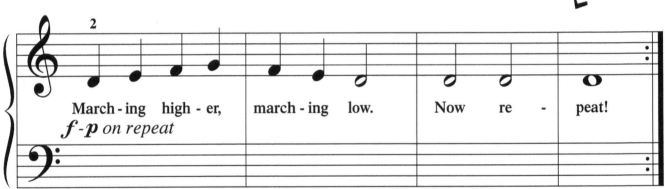

March-ing high-er, march-ing low. Now re - peat!
f-p on repeat

DAY 5: March on D-E-F

Notice the starting finger.

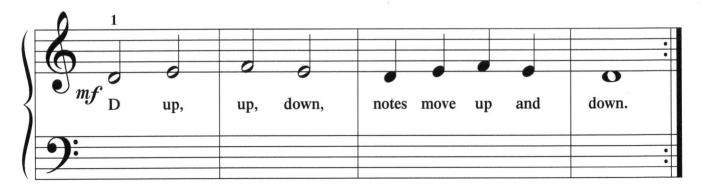

mf D up, up, down, notes move up and down.

DAY 6: March on D-E-F

mf Notes go up, notes go down, notes re - peat.

Look at me, look at me, look at me sight - read!

Congratulations, Sightreader. You are marching through the book!

Write the note name in each cloud above the music.

We're rooting for you!

Please, let's quiet down.

DAY 1: The Dance Band

DON'T
PRACTICE
THIS!

Notice the L.H. starting finger.

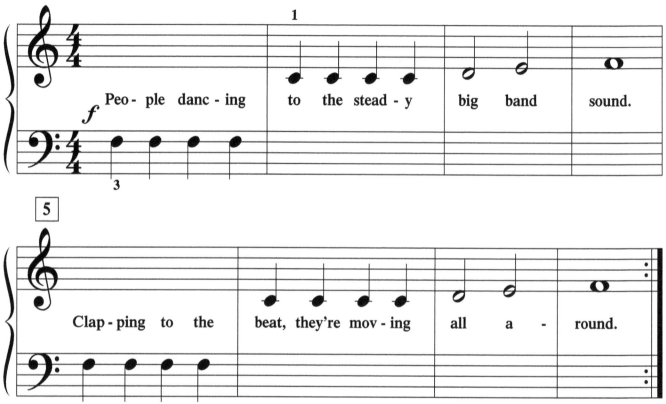

DAY 2: The Dance Band

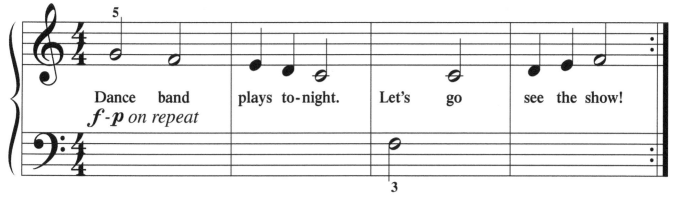

DAY 3: The Dance Band

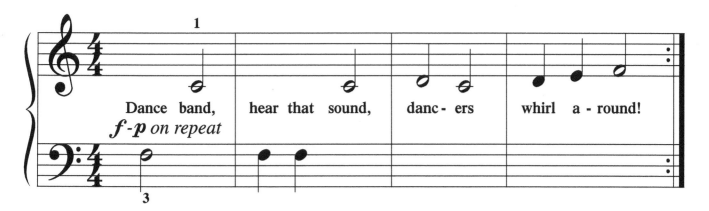

DAY 4: The Dance Band

DON'T PRACTICE THIS!

Notice the L.H. starting finger.

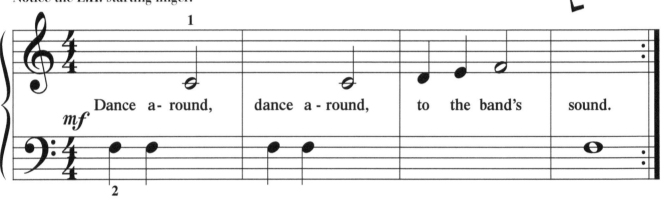

DAY 5: The Dance Band

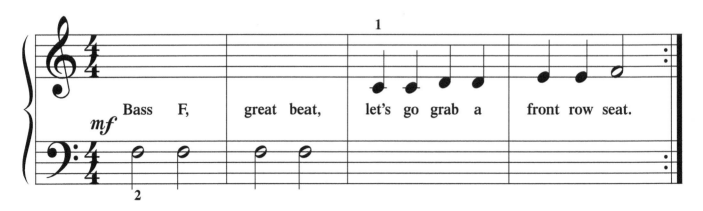

DAY 6: The Dance Band

Hip, hip, hoo - ray, (2 - 3 - 4) con - cert to - day. (2 - 3 - 4)

Hear the drums play. (2 - 3 - 4) Hip, hip, hoo - ray! (2 - 3 - 4)

Well done, Sightreader! You helped Little Treble and Little Bass win!

WE WON! WE WON!

Write each note name in the guitars above the music.

DAY 1: Frogs on Logs

Notice the starting finger.

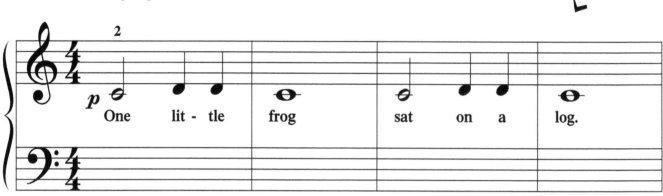

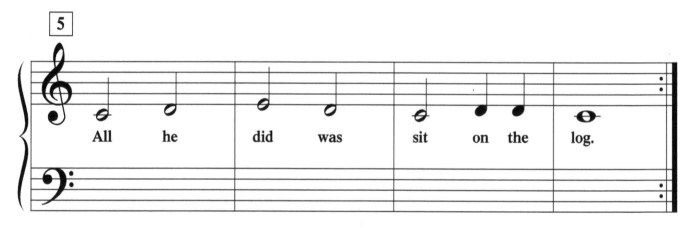

DAY 2: Frogs on Logs

DAY 3: Frogs on Logs

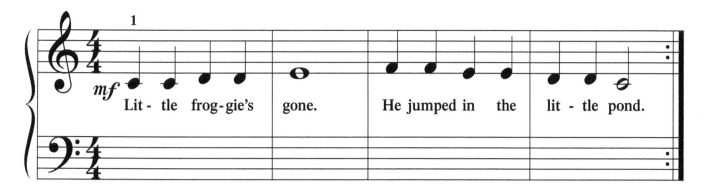

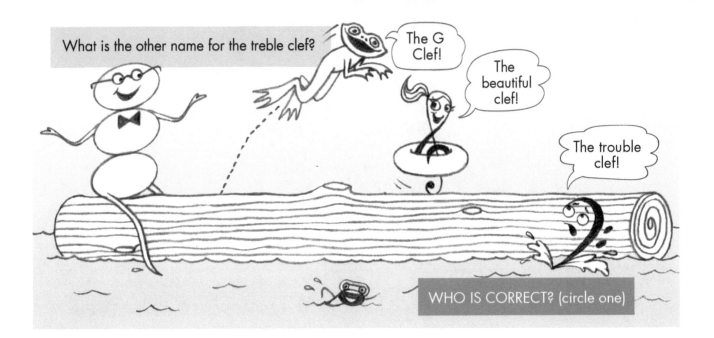

DAY 4: Frogs on Logs

Can you hop finger 2 up the keys?

DON'T PRACTICE THIS!

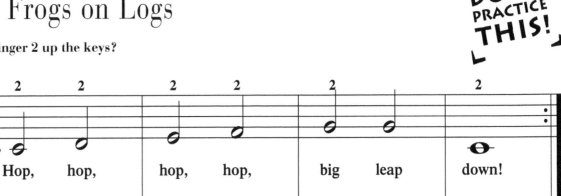

Hop, hop, hop, hop, big leap down!

DAY 5: Frogs on Logs

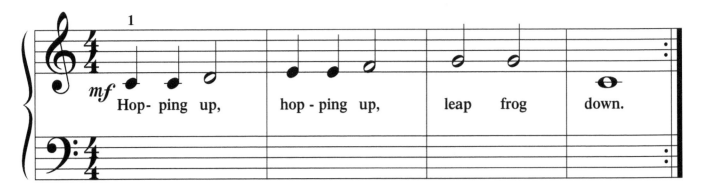

Hop-ping up, hop-ping up, leap frog down.

DAY 6: Frogs on Logs

Notice the finger change at measure 5.

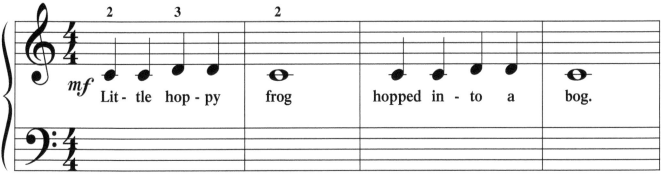

Lit - tle hop - py | frog | hopped in - to a | bog.

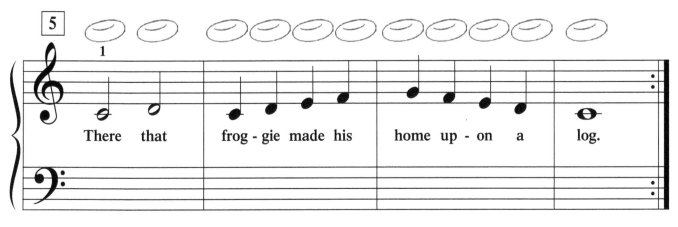

There that | frog - gie made his | home up - on a | log.

Write the note name in each inner tube above the music.

DAY 1: Let's Play Ball!

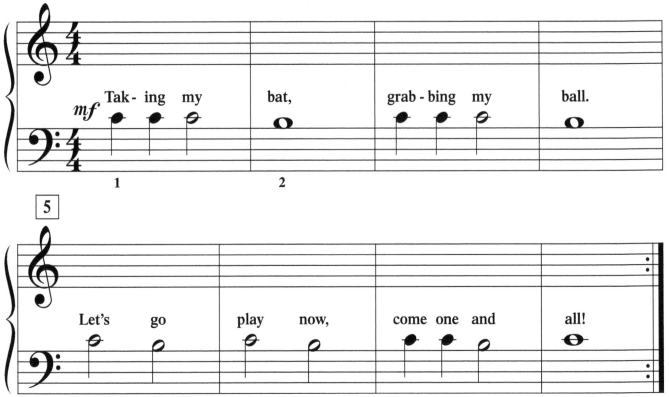

B is for Ball! Scan the music. How many **space note B's** do you see?

CAN YOU ANSWER THE QUESTION? (circle one)
2 B's   3 B's   4 B's   5 B's

DAY 2: Let's Play Ball!

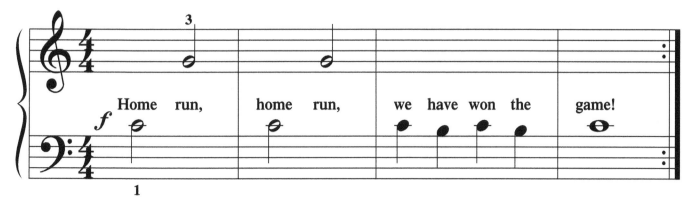

DAY 3: Let's Play Ball!

Notice the R.H. starting finger.

DAY 4: Let's Play Ball!

Notice the R.H. starting finger.

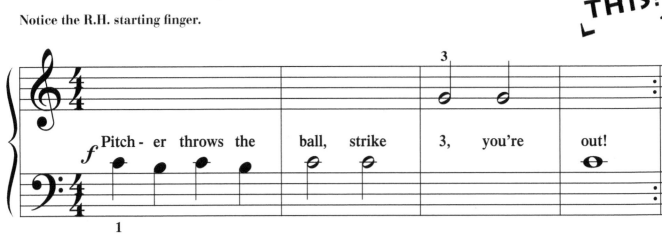

DAY 5: Let's Play Ball!

DAY 6: Let's Play Ball!

Notice the R.H. starting finger.

DAY 1: Rodeo

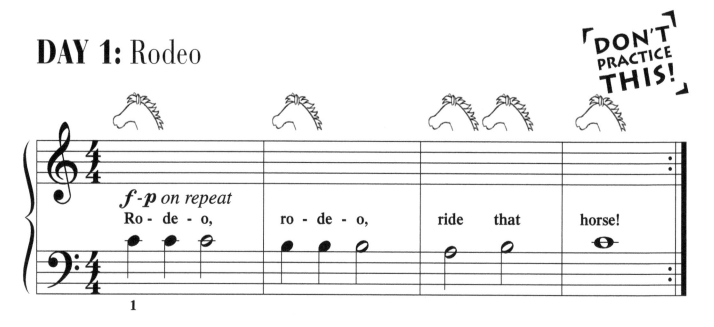

DAY 2: Rodeo

Notice the R.H. starting finger.

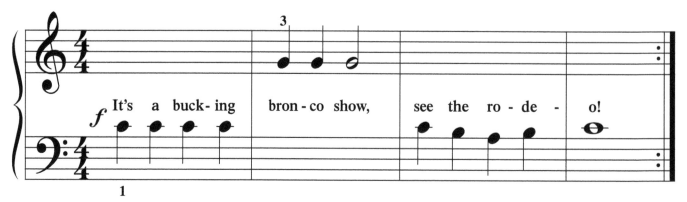

DAY 3: Rodeo

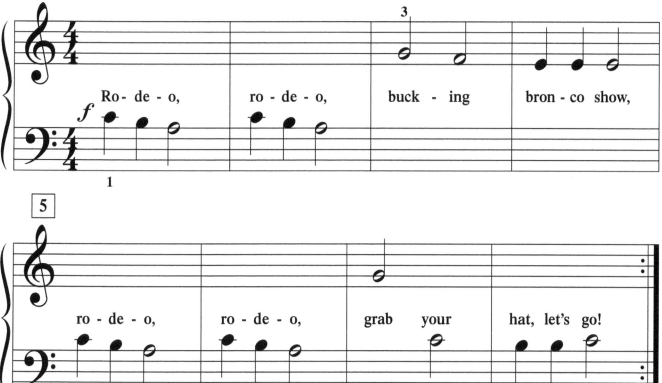

DAY 4: Rodeo

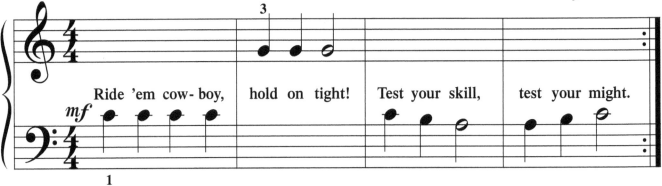

Ride 'em cow-boy, hold on tight! Test your skill, test your might.

DAY 5: Rodeo

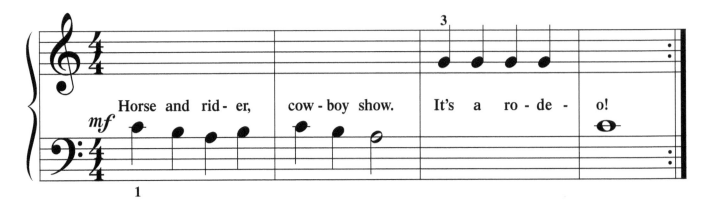

Horse and rid-er, cow-boy show. It's a ro-de-o!

DAY 6: Rodeo

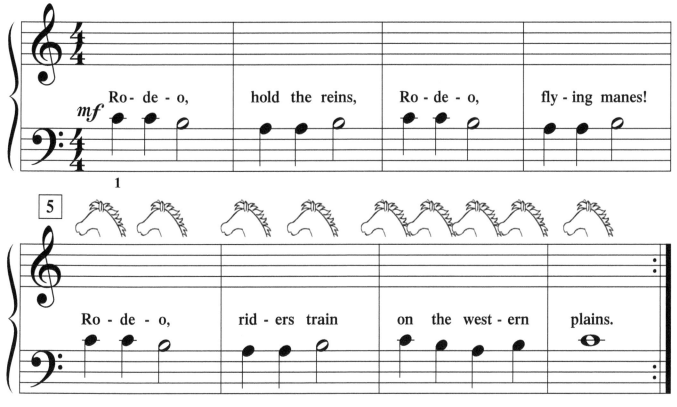

Congratulations, Sightreader.
You made it to **DAY 6** at the rodeo!

We love the rodeo!

Shh…

WRITE THE NOTE NAMES ON THE HORSE HEADS ABOVE.

DAY 1: Come See the Parade!

DON'T PRACTICE THIS!

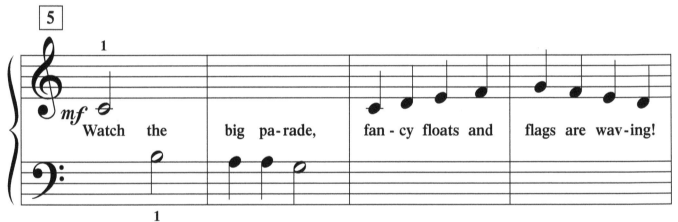

DAY 2: Come See the Parade!

Notice the L.H. starting finger.

DON'T PRACTICE THIS!

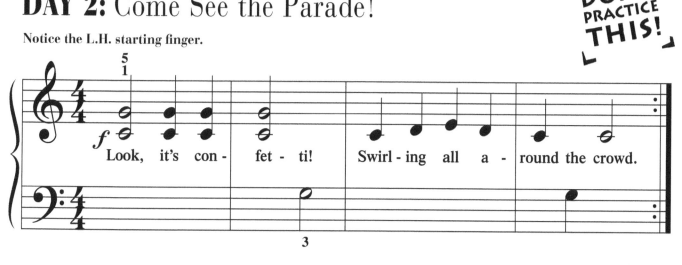

Look, it's con - fet - ti! Swirl - ing all a - round the crowd.

DAY 3: Come See the Parade!

Big go - ril - la float in the pa - rade!

Write the note names in the clouds above the music.

Write the note names in each bluebird below.

DAY 4: Come See the Parade!

DON'T PRACTICE THIS!

mf Who is com-ing next now? Mis-ter Blue-bird's here!

DAY 5: Come See the Parade!

mf Come and see the big pa-rade, we've saved a front row seat for you!

DAY 6: Come See the Parade!

You have made it to DAY 6. Way to go!

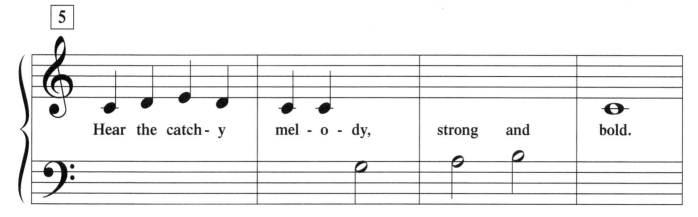

Hear the catch-y mel-o-dy, strong and bold.

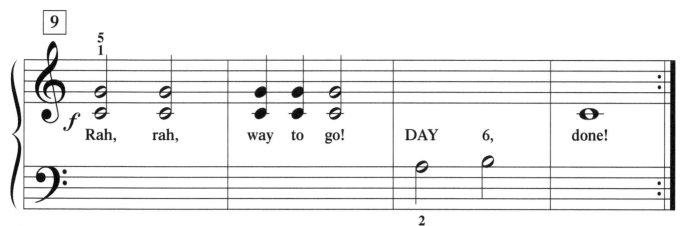

Rah, rah, way to go! DAY 6, done!

DAY 6!

WAY TO GO!

Tweet! How is the music in Line 2 different than Line 1? Tell your teacher.

49

DAY 1: Hey, Hey, Look at Me!

DAY 2: Hey, Hey, Look at Me!

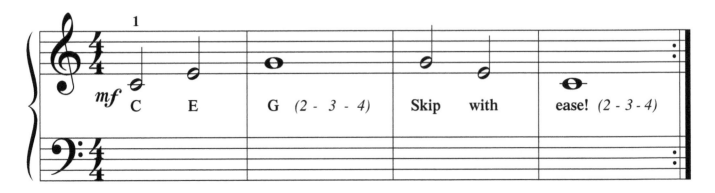

DAY 3: Hey, Hey, Look at Me!

DON'T PRACTICE THIS!

Train your eyes, this is wise, train your eyes, you'll be wise!

DAY 4: Hey, Hey, Look at Me!

C E G   G E C   Hey, hey, hey,   look at me!

DAY 5: Hey, Hey, Look at Me!

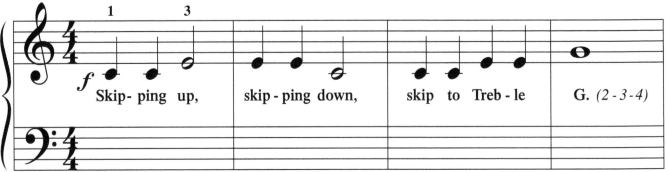

Skip- ping up,   skip- ping down,   skip to Treb - le   G. *(2 - 3 - 4)*

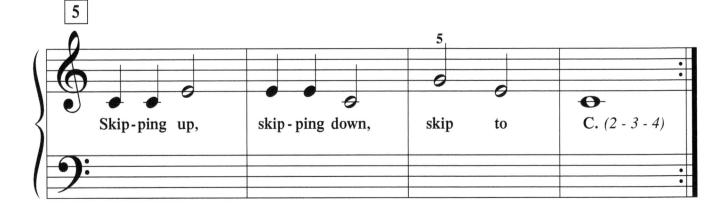

Skip-ping up,   skip - ping down,   skip   to   C. *(2 - 3 - 4)*

Look carefully! Which little birds are skipping?

Tweet!

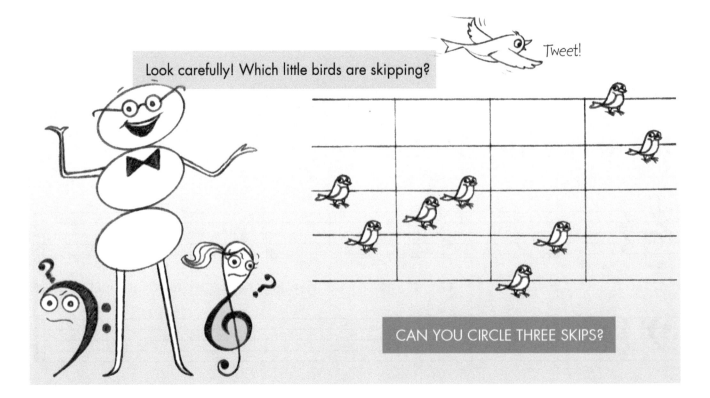

CAN YOU CIRCLE THREE SKIPS?

DAY 6: Hey, Hey, Look at Me!

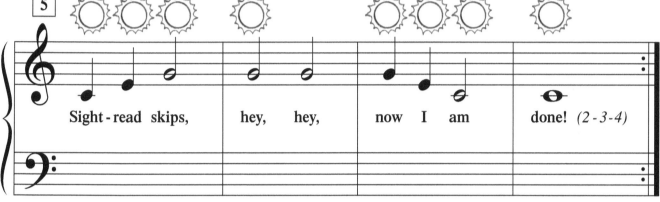

Sight- read skips, hey, hey, skip - ping is fun. *(2 - 3 - 4)*
f-p on repeat

Sight - read skips, hey, hey, now I am done! *(2-3-4)*

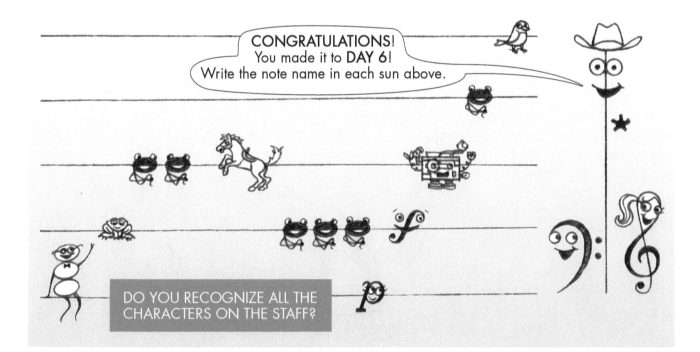

CONGRATULATIONS!
You made it to **DAY 6**!
Write the note name in each sun above.

DO YOU RECOGNIZE ALL THE CHARACTERS ON THE STAFF?

DAY 1: Elephant Ride

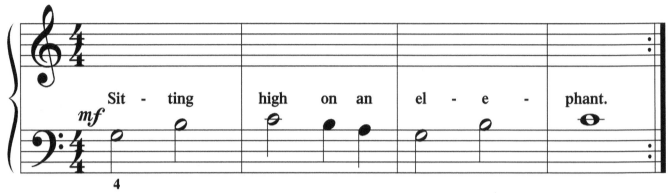

DAY 2: Elephant Ride

Hey Sightreader! Fill in the blanks. A SKIP goes from a line to a _____ or a space to a _____.

Hello down there!

Hello!

54

DAY 3: Elephant Ride

DAY 4: Elephant Ride

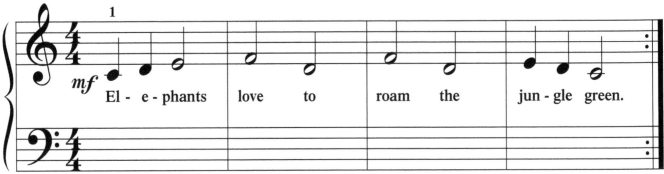

DAY 5: Elephant Ride

DAY 6: Elephant Ride

DON'T PRACTICE THIS!

Sit - ting ver - y high, I can touch the sky,

mf

when I'm on an el - e - phant pass - ing by.

Congratulations, Sightreader!

Wow! We're reading skips!

Write the note names in the elephants above.

Hello down there!

Shh!

DAY 1: Yankee Doodle

DON'T PRACTICE THIS!

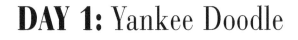

DAY 2: Yankee Doodle

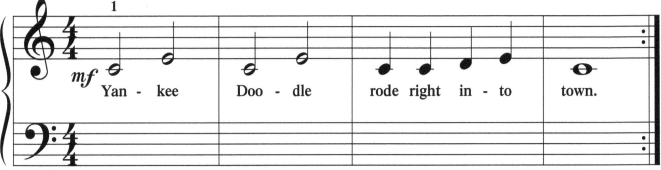

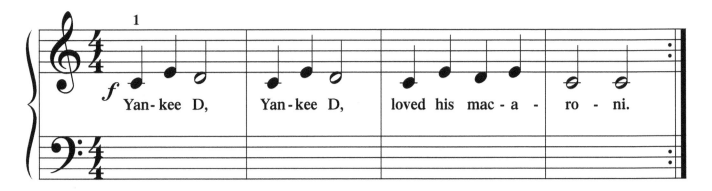

DAY 3: Yankee Doodle

Notice the L.H. starting finger.

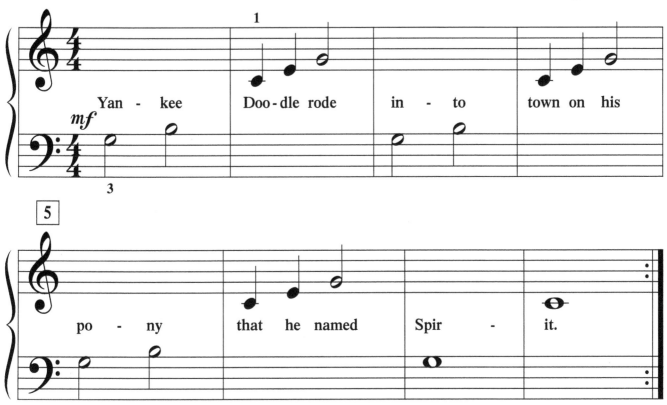

Yan - kee | Doo - dle rode | in - to | town on his
po - ny | that he named | Spir - | it.

Little Treble and Little Bass, how many times does this melody appear?

3 times?

4 times?

WHO IS RIGHT?
(circle one)

Name the notes in the ice cream cones below.

DAY 4: Yankee Doodle

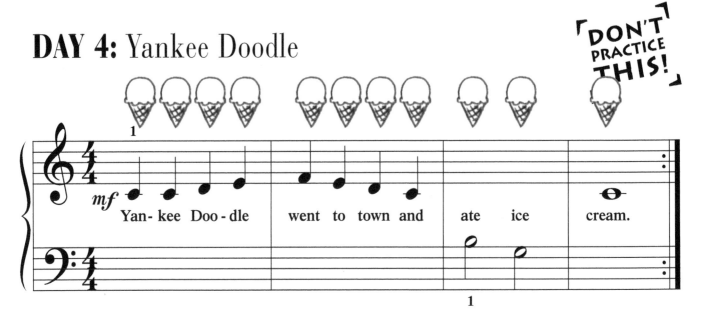

DAY 5: Yankee Doodle

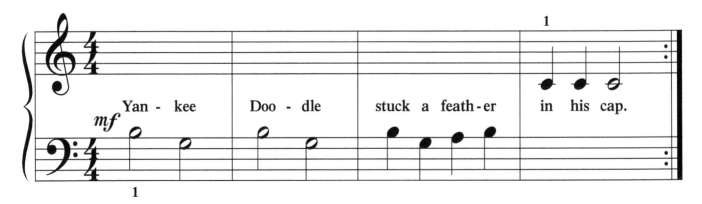

DAY 6: Yankee Doodle

DAY 1: A Joke for You

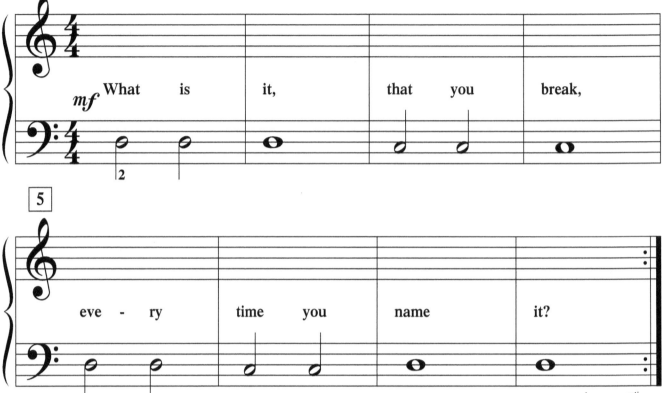

In the bass clef, the middle line is D.
"Hey, diddle, diddle, D's in the middle."

What is it, that you break,

every time you name it?

Answer: Silence

Little Treble and Little Bass,
please circle the correct Bass C's.
(Hint: SPACE 2 and the stem goes up.)

Coming...

Just one more joke.

CAN YOU CIRCLE THE CORRECT C's?

DAY 2: A Joke for You

Notice the L.H. starting finger.

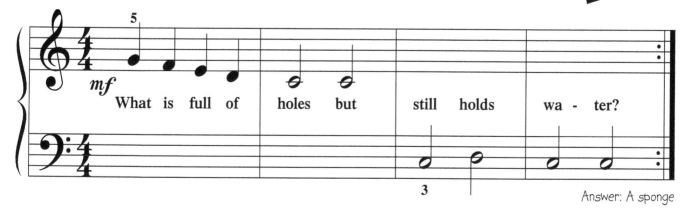

Answer: A sponge

DAY 3: A Joke for You

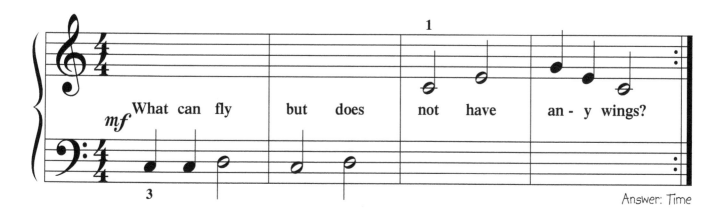

Answer: Time

DAY 4: A Joke for You

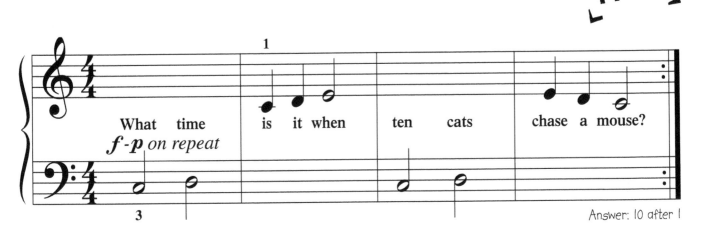

Answer: 10 after I

DAY 5: A Joke for You

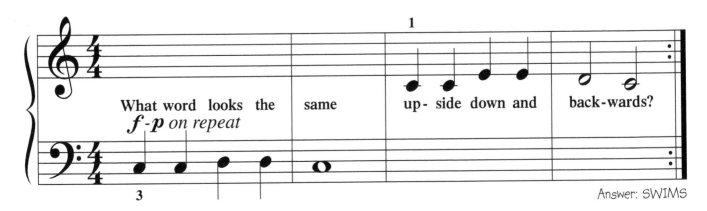

Answer: SWIMS

DAY 6: A Joke for You

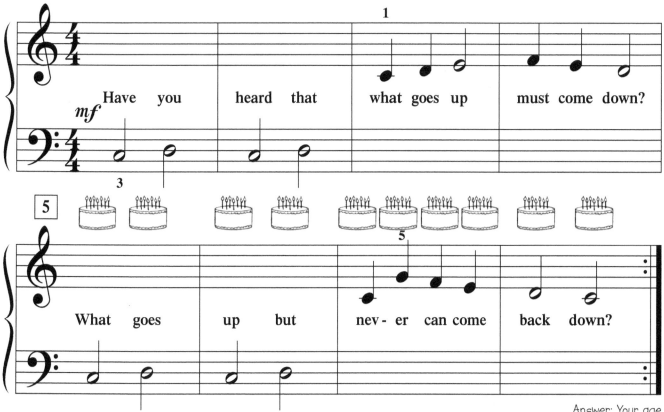

Have you heard that what goes up must come down?

What goes up but nev-er can come back down?

Answer: Your age

SURPRISE!
Happy Birthday, Penny Piano!

Oh, thank you!

Write the note names in the cakes above.

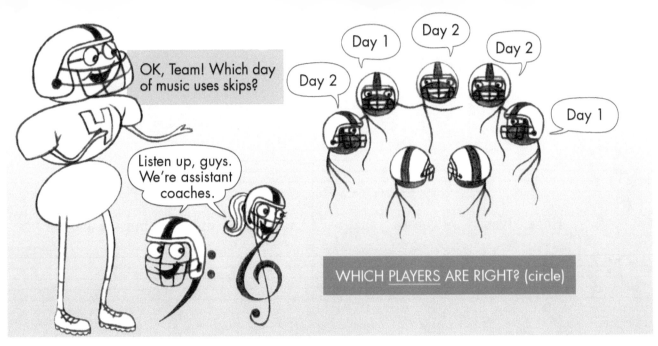

DAY 1: Football Game

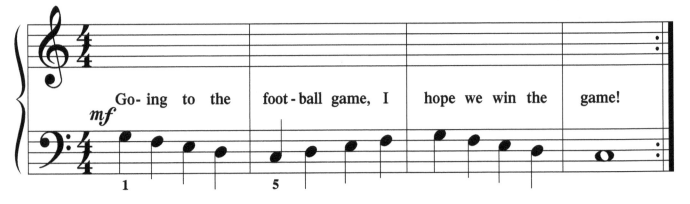

DAY 2: Football Game

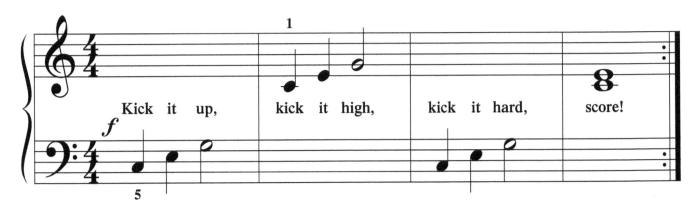

DAY 3: Football Game

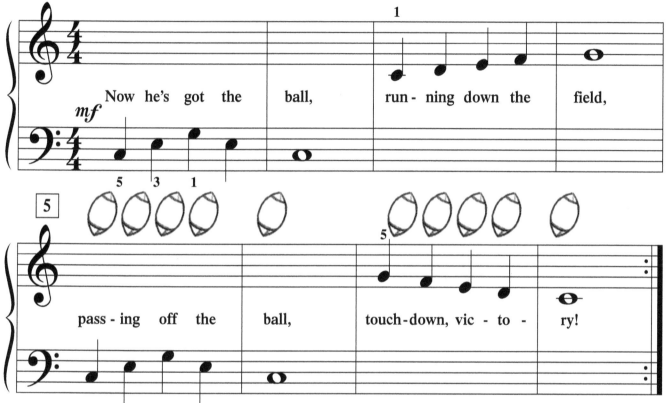

Write the note names in each football above.

Go! Go! Go! Go! Go!

Catch it, Porter!

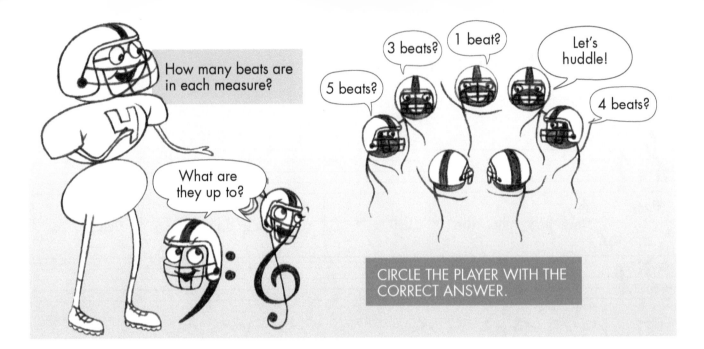

DAY 4: Football Game

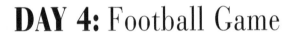

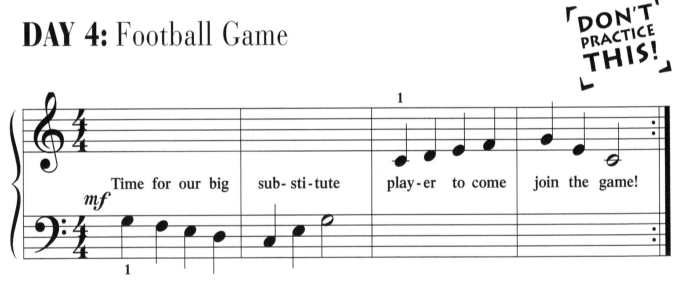

DAY 5: Football Game

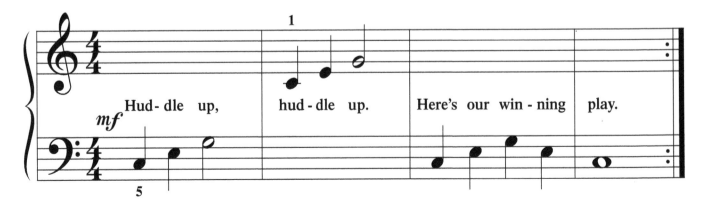

DAY 6: Football Game

DAY 1: Copy Cat

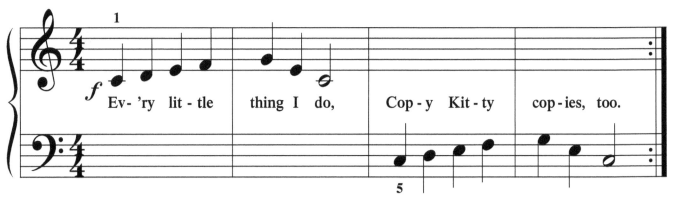

DAY 2: Copy Cat

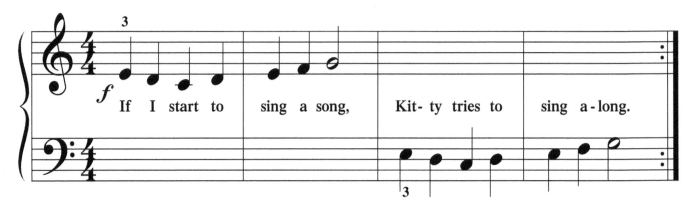

DON'T PRACTICE THIS!

DAY 3: Copy Cat

Cop - y Kit - ty's great. She can im - i - tate!

DAY 4: Copy Cat

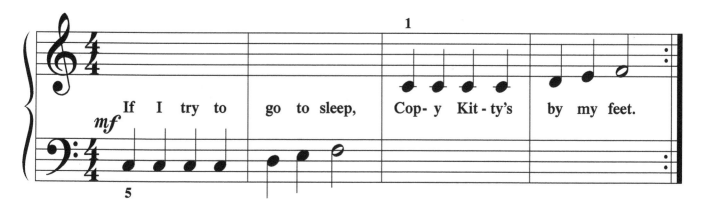

If I try to go to sleep, Cop- y Kit - ty's by my feet.

DAY 5: Copy Cat

Three examples are skipping.
Can you circle them?

C - E - G
D - E - F
G - E - C
F - D - C
F - D - F

CAN YOU CIRCLE THE THREE SKIPS?

72

DAY 6: Copy Cat

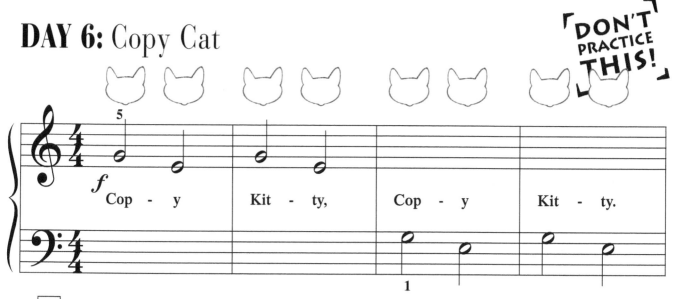

DAY 1: Grandmother

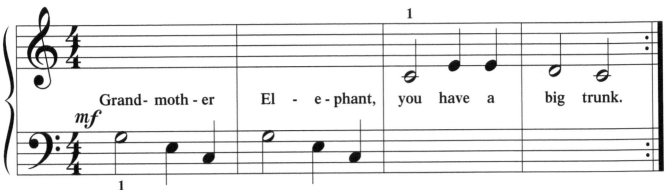

DAY 2: Grandmother

DAY 3: Grandmother

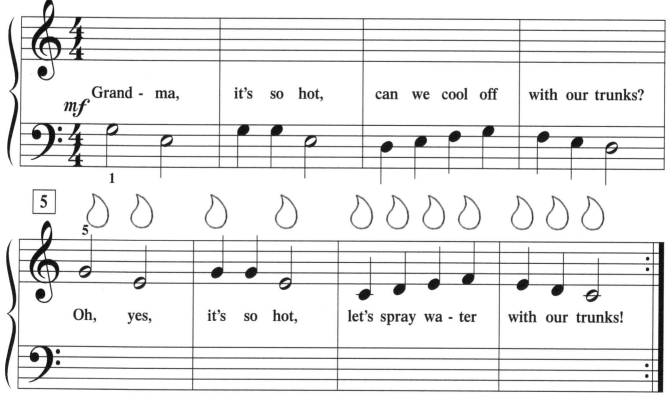

Grand - ma, it's so hot, can we cool off with our trunks?

Oh, yes, it's so hot, let's spray wa - ter with our trunks!

Use your trunk to cool off, little one!

TRUE or FALSE?
(circle one)
DAY 3 is a musical
question and answer.

That baby is SO cute!

This is fun, Grandma!

WRITE THE NOTE NAMES IN THE WATER DROPS ABOVE.

DAY 4: Grandmother

Notice the L.H. starting finger.

DON'T PRACTICE THIS!

mf Grand - ma, slide with me, Grand - ma, here we go!

DAY 5: Grandmother

mf Grand - moth - er, climb - ing up, Grand - moth - er, slid - ing down.

Which two examples are skipping?

1.
2.
3.

Examples 2 and 3?

Examples 1 and 2?

Examples 1 and 3?

WHO IS RIGHT? (circle one)

DAY 6: Grandmother

77

DAY 1: Lemonade Stand

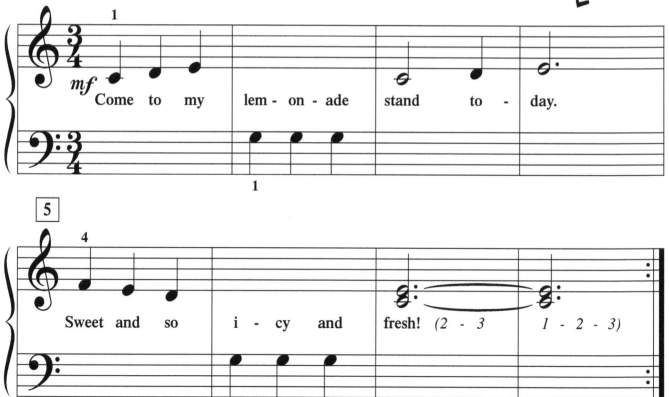

DAY 2: Lemonade Stand

DON'T PRACTICE THIS!

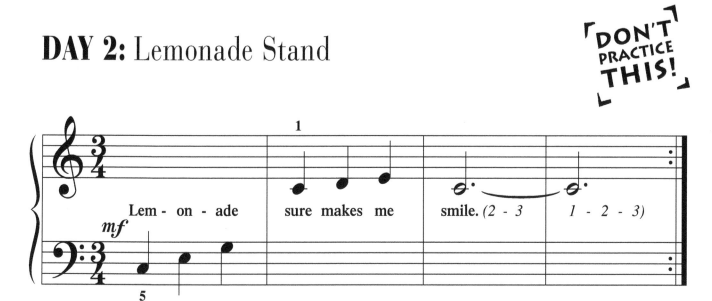

DAY 3: Lemonade Stand

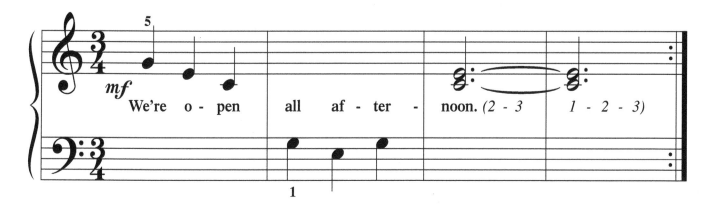

DAY 4: Lemonade Stand

DON'T PRACTICE THIS!

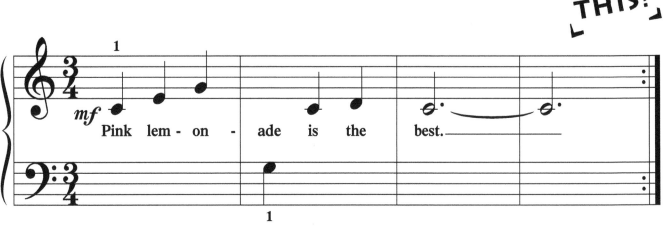

DAY 5: Lemonade Stand

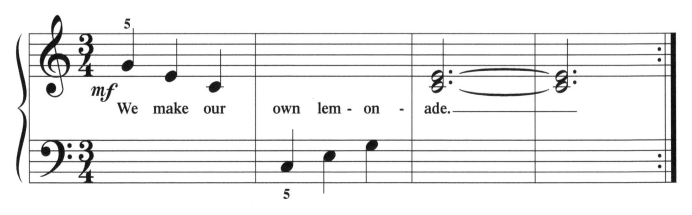

DAY 1: All My Friends

Think: Hey, diddle, diddle, D's in the middle.

DAY 2: All My Friends

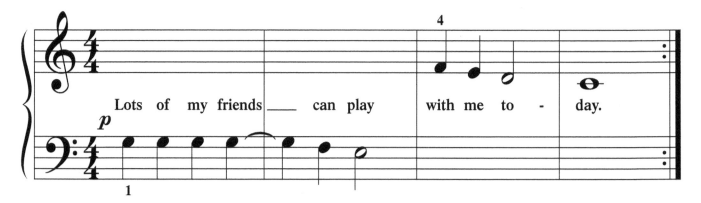

DAY 3: All My Friends

Write the note name in each sun above.

DAY 4: All My Friends

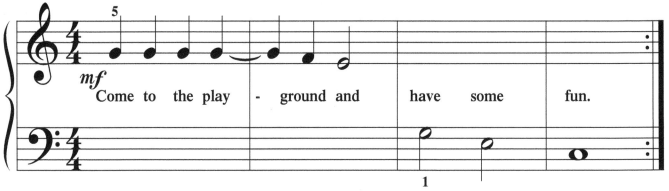

DAY 5: All My Friends

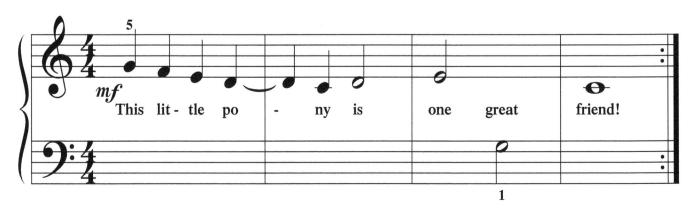

DAY 6: All My Friends

HAVE FUN NAMING EACH CHARACTER.

DAY 1: Princess or Monster?

DAY 2: Princess or Monster?

How many measures in DAY 2 have a rest on BEAT 3?

She's a real princess!

Purr... 1 measure has a rest on beat 3.

ROAR! I say 2 measures!

Wow! A real monster!

WHO IS CORRECT? (circle one)

DAY 3: Princess or Monster?

Write the note names in the leaves above.

My new friend is a princess!

My new friend is a super monster!

DAY 4: Princess or Monster?

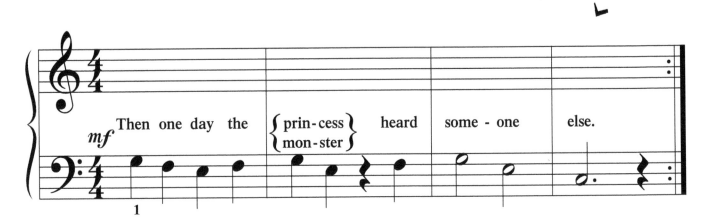

DAY 5: Princess or Monster?

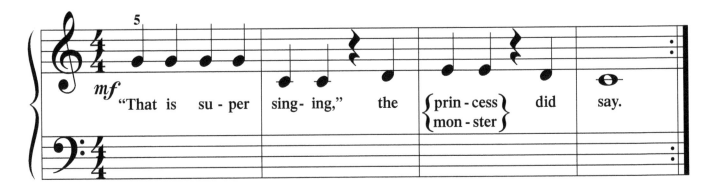

DAY 6: Princess or Monster?

DAY 1: The Bugle Boys

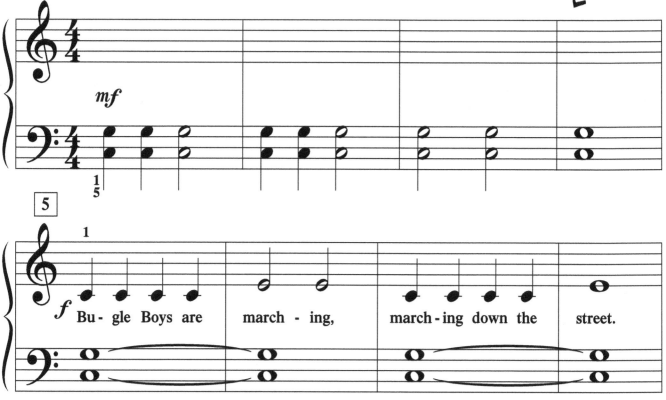

DAY 2: The Bugle Boys

Write the note names in each bugle above.

Squeal! 5 more days to go!

Two Little Bugle Boys playing their horns...

DAY 3: The Bugle Boys

DAY 4: The Bugle Boys

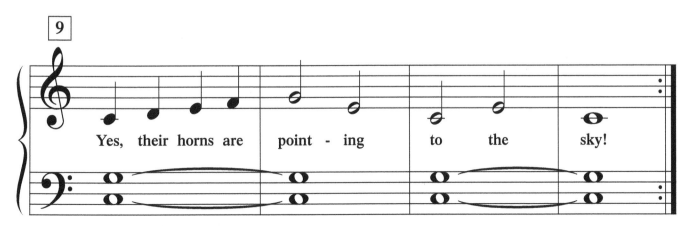

DAY 5: The Bugle Boys

f Hear the bu- glers play their fan - cy tunes.

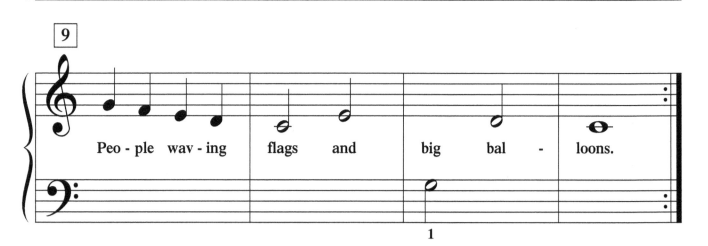

Peo - ple wav- ing flags and big bal - loons.

DAY 6: The Bugle Boys

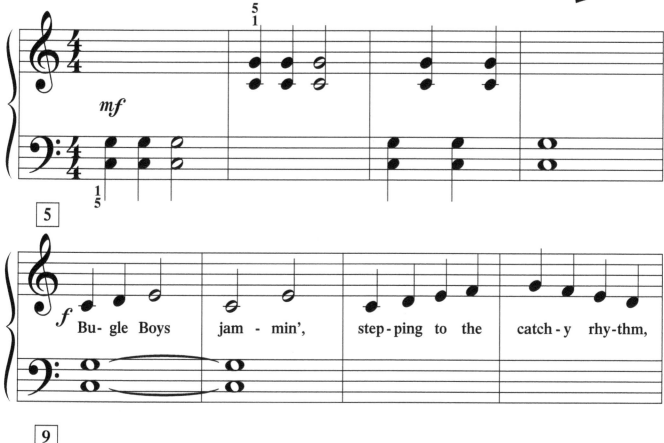

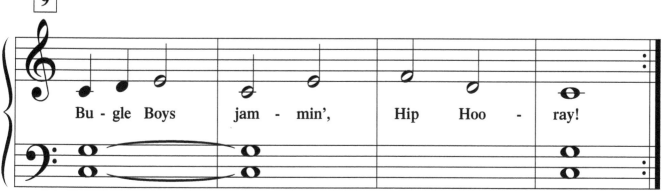

THIS IS IT! CONGRATULATIONS, SIGHTREADER!

Six Little Bugle Boys playing their horns!

Wait for me! I'm number 7.

SIGN THE CERTIFICATE ON P. 96

Piano Adventures® Certificate
CONGRATULATIONS

_____
(Your Name)

You are now a Primer Sightreader. Keep up the great work!

_____
Teacher

_____
Date

V102022